Colonial & Revolution Songbook

with historical commentary

Compiled and edited by Keith & Rusty McNeil

Companion to the recording
Colonial & Revolution Songs with historical narration

WEM Records
Riverside, California

also by Keith & Rusty McNeil

Recordings

American History Through Folksong
    Colonial & Revolution Songs with historical narration
    Moving West Songs with historical narration
    Civil War Songs with historical narration
    Cowboy Songs with historical narration
    Western Railroad Songs with historical narration
    Working & Union Songs with historical narration

Singing the Holiday Season
Folksongs for Children
Coarse & Fine

ISBN 1-878360-08-6

Contents

All songs, unless otherwise specified and credited,
are traditional songs arranged and adapted by Keith & Rusty McNeil.

Colonial America, 17th Century

Seal of New England

The Girl I Left Behind Me

Europeans had settled the New England coast by about 1630, a time when the arts were very sophisticated in Britain and on the European continent. They were dancing the ballet in France, producing opera in Italy, and singing madrigals in England. However, the people who came to America – adventurers, explorers, farmers, sailors, missionaries, slaves, noblemen and indentured servants – did not have time for opera, ballet or madrigals, they were too busy attempting to survive in a new land. The kind of music brought to America in those early days were folk songs and ballads.

One of these was "The Girl I Left Behind Me," a song popular in Ireland and England since Elizabethan times, and an American favorite for more than 300 years. America's soldiers sang it, marched to it, and wrote parodies of it. This is the Irish version.

The Girl I Left Behind Me

Words and music: anonymous.

I'm lone-some since I crossed the hill, and o'er the moor and va-ley, Such hea-vy thoughts my heart do fill, Since part-ing with my Sal-ly. I seek no more the fine and gay, for each but does re-mind me, How swift the hours did pass a-way, With the girl I left be-hind me.

I'm lonesome since I crossed the hill, and o'er the moor and valley,
Such heavy thoughts my heart do fill, since parting with my Sally.
I seek no more the fine and gay, for each but does remind me,
How swift the hours did pass away, with the girl I left behind me.

Oh, ne'er shall I forget the night, the stars were bright above me,
And gently lent their silvery light, when first she vowed she loved me.
But now I'm bound for Brighton camp, kind heaven may favor find me,
And send me safely back again, to the girl I left behind me.

The bee shall honey taste no more, the dove become a ranger,
The dashing waves shall cease to roar, e'er she's to me a stranger.
The vows we've registered above me, shall ever cheer and bind me
In constancy to her I love, the girl I left behind me.

The Golden Vanity

Most of the songs that came to America were not written down, but some were printed on broad sheets of paper and were called broadsides.

One of the more colorful figures in early American history was poet, writer, explorer, businessman Sir Walter Raleigh. He named Virginia, helped introduce potato and tobacco plants to Ireland, established an unsuccessful colony on Roanoke Island in North Carolina, helped defeat the Spanish Armada and lost his head in the Tower of London. While Raleigh gained fame for his courtesy to Queen Elizabeth, he gained infamy among his sailors for his cruelty. The ballad "The Golden Vanity" was originally a broadside called "Sir Walter Raleigh Sailing in the Lowlands," and the ship was called "The Sweet Trinity." Over the years, the Sweet Trinity became "The Golden Vanity."

"The Golden Vanity" appears as ballad number 286 in Francis James Child's classic collection "The English and Scottish Popular Ballads." The ballad has many other variants, including "The French Galley," "The Lowlands Low," and "The Turkish Galley."

Sir Walter Raleigh

The Golden Vanity

Words and music: anonymous.

There was a ship that sailed all on the low-land sea, And the name of our ship was the Gol-den Van-i-ty, And we feared she would be ta-ken by the Span-ish en-e-my, As we sailed up-on the low-land, low-land low, We sailed up-on the low-land sea.

There was a ship that sailed all on the lowland sea,
And the name of our ship was the Golden Vanity,
And we feared she would be taken by the Spanish enemy,
As we sailed upon the lowland, lowland low,
We sailed upon the lowland sea.

Then up stepped our cabin boy and boldly outspoke he,
And he said to our captain, "What will you give to me,
If I'll swim alongside of the Spanish enemy
And sink her in the lowland, lowland low,
And sink her in the lowland sea?"

Well, I will give you silver, and I will give you gold,
And my fair young daughter your bonnie bride shall be,
If you'll swim alongside of the Spanish enemy
And sink her in the lowland, lowland low,
And sink her in the lowland sea.

So the boy he made him ready, and overboard sprang he,
And he swam alongside of the Spanish enemy,
And with his brace and auger in her side he bored holes three,
And he sank her in the lowland, lowland low,
He sank her in the lowland sea.

Then quickly he swam back to the cheering of the crew,
But the captain would not heed him, for his promise he did rue,
And he scorned his bold entreaty, as loudly he did sue,
And he left him in the lowland, lowland low,
He left him in the lowland sea.

Then round about he turned and he swam to the port side,
And up unto his messmates, most bitterly he cried,
"Oh, messmates pull me up, for I'm drifting with the tide
And I'm sinking in the lowland, lowland low,
I'm sinking in the lowland sea."

So his messmates drew him up, but on the deck he died,
And we stitched him in his hammock which was so deep and wide,
And we lowered him overboard, and he drifted with the tide,
And he sank into the lowland, lowland low,
He sank into the lowland sea.

We Gather Together

The English, Spanish, Dutch, French, Swedish, German, Irish and Scots colonists encountered a number of nations already living on the American continent: Seneca, Cayuga, Onondaga, Oneida, Delaware, Mohawk, Algonquin, Natchez, Creek, Chickasaw, Choctaw, Cherokee. Reactions of the Native Americans to the Europeans, and vice versa, varied from fear and anger to curiosity and friendly cooperation. Early contact with Native Americans by traders and adventurers proved to be of great value to the pilgrims. At least two of the Native Americans who showed the pilgrims how to survive the fierce New England winters spoke English, and taught survival skills to the new settlers, making possible the famous Thanksgiving celebration of December 13, 1621.

This song was published in the Netherlands by Adrianus Valerius in 1621. Five years later Dutch settlers brought it to New Amsterdam on Manhattan Island. In America today, after nearly four centuries, the song continues its timeless appeal.

We Gather Together

Words and music: anonymous.

We gath-er to-geth-er to ask the Lord's bless-ing, He chas-tens and has-tens His will to make known. The wick-ed op-press-ing now cease to be dis-tress-ing, Sing prais-es to His name for He for-gets not His own.

We gather together to ask the Lord's blessing,
He chastens and hastens His will to make known.
The wicked oppressing now cease to be distressing,
Sing praises to His name for He forgets not His own.

Beside us to guide us our God with us joining,
Ordaining, maintaining His kingdom divine.
So from the beginning the fighting we were winning,
Thou Lord wast at our side and all the glory be Thine.

We all do extoll Thee, Thou leader triumphant,
And pray that Thou still our defender wilt be,
Let Thy congregation escape all tribulation,
Thy name be ever praised in glory, Lord make us free.

Old Hundredth

In Massachusetts Bay Colony in the 1650s, a Puritan wedding feast would likely begin with wine and prayer, followed by a variety of game, fish, fowl and vegetables, washed down with beer, cider, brandy, wine, flip (a hot spiced drink made of beer), ale and cider, and sack possett (milk, curdled with strong, dry wine). After dinner the singing would begin. The only religious songs sung by the Puritans were psalms, sung to a lively tempo. The favorite was the hundredth psalm, and they called it "Old Hundredth." The Puritans might have sung the version of

"Old Hundredth" from the Ainsworth Psalter, printed in 1621, which the Pilgrims brought from Holland:

> *Shout to Jehovah, all the earth;*
> *Serve Ye Jehovah with gladness;*
> *Before Him come with singing mirth;*
> *Know that Jehovah He God is.*

It is more likely, however, that they sang the version from the Geneva Psalter, published in 1551.

Old Hundredth

Words and music: anonymous.

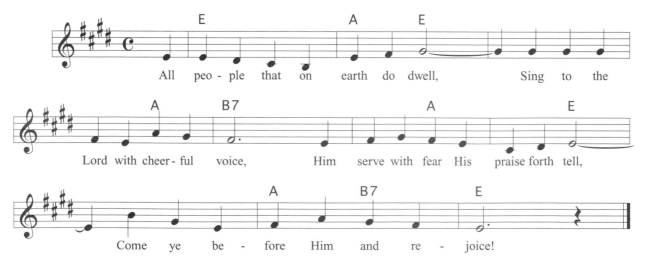

All people that on earth do dwell, Sing to the Lord with cheerful voice, Him serve with fear His praise forth tell, Come ye before Him and rejoice!

All people that on earth do dwell,
Sing to the Lord with cheerful voice,
Him serve with fear His praise forth tell,
Come ye before Him and rejoice!

Oh, enter then His gates with praise,
Approach with joy His courts unto,
Praise, laud and bless His name always,
For it is seemly for to do.

The Willow Tree

New Englanders sang secular songs, too. England had a strong singing tradition, and New Englanders carried on that tradition. The old English ballad "Lady Isabel and the Elf Knight" (ballad number 4 in Francis James Child's collection) is the type of song sung in 17th century New England. The ballad, which recounts the Bluebeard story, was one of the most widely circulated of all the traditional ballads, with variants in Northern and Southern Europe as well as in America. "The Willow Tree" is an early American version. Ballads served as escape literature for Colonial Americans. It was the women who kept most of the ballads alive. Women in the colonies faced severe hardships and sexual repression, and many of the ballads that survived expressed fantasy and wish-fulfillment from the woman's point of view. "The Willow Tree" is a good example.

The Willow Tree

Words and music: anonymous.

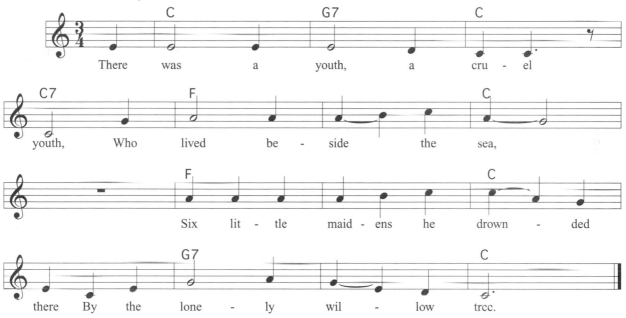

There was a youth, a cru - el youth, Who lived be - side the sea, Six lit - tle maid - ens he drown - ded there By the lone - ly wil - low tree.

There was a youth, a cruel youth,
Who lived beside the sea,
Six little maidens he drownded there
By the lonely willow tree.

As he walked o'er with Sally Brown,
As he walked o'er with she,
An evil thought came to him there,
By the lonely willow tree.

"Oh turn your back to the water's side,
And face the willow tree,
Six little maidens I've drownded here,
And you the seventh shall be."

"Take off, take off your golden gown,
Take off your gown," cried he.
"For though I am going to murder you
I would not spoil your finery."

"Oh, turn around you false young man,
Oh turn around," cried she,
"For 'tis not meet that such a youth
A naked woman should see."

He turned around, that false young man,
And faced the willow tree,
And seizing him boldly in both her arms,
She threw him into the sea.

"Lie there, lie there, you false young man,
Lie there, lie there," cried she,
"Six little maidens you've drownded here,
Now keep them company!"

He sank beneath the icy waves,
He sank down into the sea,
And no living thing wept a tear for him,
Save the lonely willow tree.

The Great Silkie of Sule Skerry

Immigrants from the Scots Hebrides and the Shetland and Orkney Islands brought tales of silkies or sealmen. Silkies were believed to be enchanted creatures who live beneath the sea but occasionally take off their sealskins and walk on land as ordinary men. If they lose their sealskins, they can no longer return home, and become subject to the power of humans. Silkies are sometimes called "finns." This ballad (Child ballad number 113) comes from the Shetland Islands.

The Great Silkie of Sule Skerry

Words and music: anonymous.

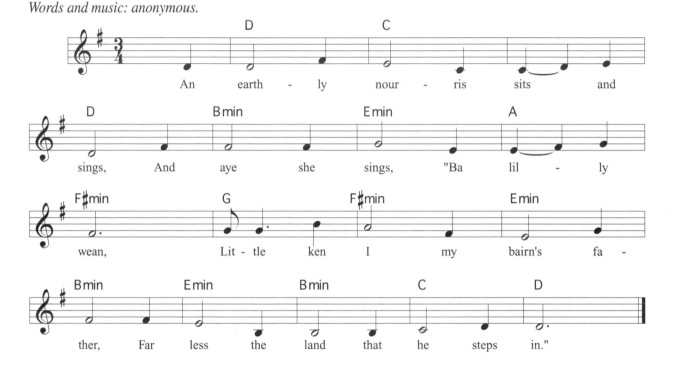

An earthly nourris sits and sings,
And aye she sings, "Ba lilly wean,
Little ken I my bairn's father,
Far less the land that he steps in."

Then in steps he to her bed-fit,
And a grumly guest I'm sure was he,
Saying, "Here am I, thy bairn's father,
Although I be not comely."

"I am a man upon the land,
And I am a silkie in the sea,
And when I'm far and far from land,
My home it is in Sule Skerry."

"Ah, 'tis not well," the maiden cried,
"Ah, 'tis not well, alas," cried she,
"That the great silky from Sule Skerry
Should have come and brought a bairn to me."

Then he has taken a purse of gold,
And he has laid it on her knee,
Saying, "Give to me my little young son,
And take thee up thy nourris-fee."

"It shall come to pass on a summer's day,
When the sun shines hot on every stone,
That I shall take my little young son,
And teach him for to swim the foam."

"And thou shall marry a proud gunner,
And a proud gunner I'm sure he'll be,
And the very first shot that ever he'll shoot,
He'll kill both my young son and me."

"Alas, alas," the maiden cried,
"This weary fate's been laid for me,"
And then she said, and then she said,
"I'll bury me in Sule Skerry."

Jennie Jenkins

Europeans brought superstitions of various kinds to America. Columbus's sailors didn't like sailing on Friday, and they blamed goblins for torn sails and snarled running gear. Finding knives crossed on a table was bad luck, and so was spilling salt. Puritans in Massachusetts Bay Colony were deadly serious about their superstitions, especially when it came to demons, devils, wizards and witches. In the summer of 1692, in Salem, Massachusetts, they publicly hanged fourteen women and five men for witchcraft, on the testimony of five adolescent girls. The English settlers were also superstitious about colors, and these superstitions are still with us: red for sin, green for fertility, yellow for cowardice, white for purity and blue for fidelity. In England they sang color songs, and always ended the song "Jennie Jenkins" with the line "Yes, I will wear blue, for my love is true."

When the songs came to America, the symbolism began to fade. This is an early American version of "Jennie Jenkins."

Jennie Jenkins

Words and music: anonymous.

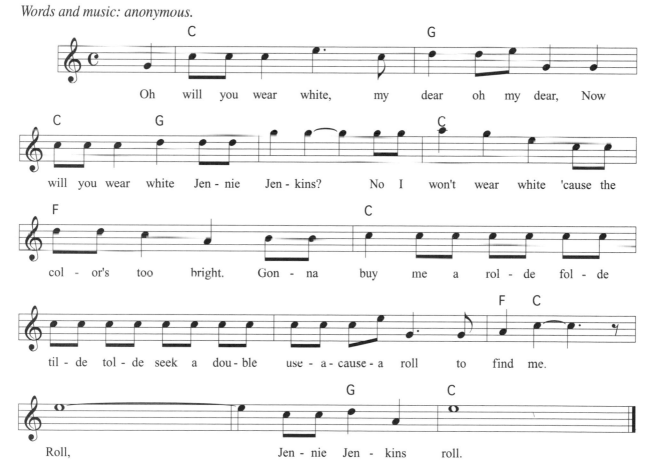

Oh will you wear white, my dear oh my dear, Now will you wear white Jennie Jenkins? No I won't wear white 'cause the color's too bright. Gonna buy me a rolde folde tilde tolde seek a double use-a-cause-a roll to find me. Roll, Jennie Jenkins roll.

Oh will you wear white, my dear oh my dear,
Now will you wear white Jennie Jenkins?
No I won't wear white 'cause the color's too bright.
Gonna buy me a rolde folde tilde tolde seek a double use-a-cause-a roll to find me.
Roll, Jennie Jenkins roll.

Will you wear green, my dear oh my dear,
Oh will you wear green Jennie Jenkins?
No I won't wear green it's a shame to be seen.
Gonna buy me a rolde folde tilde tolde seek a double use-a-cause-a roll to find me.
Roll, Jennie Jenkins roll.

Well will you wear red, my dear oh my dear,
Oh will you wear red Jennie Jenkins?
No I won't wear red it's the color of my head.
Gonna buy me (etc).

Then what will you wear, my dear oh my dear,
Oh what will you wear Jennie Jenkins?
Oh - what do you care if I just go bare?
Gonna buy me (etc).

The Trappan'd Maiden

The first shipment of tobacco from Virginia to England was sent by John Rolfe in 1613. As demands for workers on the tobacco plantations increased, more and more people sold themselves into temporary bondage to pay for passage to America. Bound to serve from three to seven years, they were often auctioned off to the highest bidder. Indentured servants had few rights, and runaways were treated harshly. By 1625, forty per cent of the people in Virginia, excluding Native Americans, were indentured servants. "The Trappan'd Maiden" was an English broadside ballad.

The Trappan'd Maiden

Words and music: anonymous.

Five years served I, under Master Guy,
In the land of Virginny-o,
Which made me for to know sorrow, grief and woe,
When that I was weary, weary, weary-o.

When my dame says go, then I must do so,
In the land of Virginny-o,
When she sits at meat, then I have none to eat,
When that I was weary, weary, weary-o.

As soon as it is day, to work I must away,
In the land of Virginny-o,
Then my dame she knocks, with her tinder box,
When that I was weary, weary, weary-o.

I have played my part, both at plow and cart,
In the land of Virginny-o,
Billets from the wood upon my back they load,
When that I was weary, weary, weary-o.

A thousand woes beside, that I do here abide,
In the land of Virginny-o,
In misery I spend my time that hath no end,
When that I was weary, weary, weary-o.

When I First Came to This Land

Pennsylvania was the most cosmopolitan of the colonies, open to all religions. Pennsylvanians assimilated religious groups rejected by the other colonies. The Germans had strong feelings about the separation of church and state, and many of them settled in Pennsylvania. German farmers, familiar with fertilization, produced high yields, exporting their surplus crops to the southern colonies and the West Indies.

Early German immigrants brought a song to Pennsylvania called "Wann Ich Mun Dem Land Rei Kumm" (When I Came to This Country). The song has many variants. This version was collected by Thomas R. Brendle and William S. Troxell.

Wann Ich Mun Dem Land Rei Kumm

Words and music: anonymous.

Wann ich mun dem Land rei kumm,
No war ich en armer Mann,
No kaf ich mire en Hinckel un fang des Hausen a.
Wann di Leid mich froje deede wie mei Hinckel heest,
Gickerigie heest mei gleines Hinkelie.

No kaf ich mir en End un fang des Hausen a,
Wann di Leid mich froje deede wie mei Endli heest,
Endli Bendli heest mei Endli,
Gickerigie heest mei gleines Hinkelie.

No kaf ich mire en Kuh un fang des Hausen a.
Wann di Leid mich frofe deede wie mei Kuh heest,
Uff un Zu heest mei Kuh,
Endli Bandli heest mei Endli,
Gicherigie heest mei gleines Hinkelie

No kaf ich mire en Genzel (etc)
Schtumm Schwenzel heest mei Genzel (etc)

No kaf ich mir en Gaul
Hawwer Maul heest mei Gaul

No kaf ich mir en Hund
Immer Gsund heest mei Hund

No kaf ich mir en Haus
Rei un Naus heest mei Haus

No grie ich mir en Fra un fang des Hausen a.
Wann di Leid mich forje deede wei mei Weiwel heest,
Hell Deiwel heest mei Weiwel,
Rei un Naus heest mei Haus,
Immer Gsund heest mei Hund,
Hawwer Maul heest mei Gaul,
Schtumm Schwenzel heest mei Genzel,
Uff un Zu heest mei Kuh,
Endli Bendli heest mei Endli,
Gicherigie heest mei gleines Hinckelie.

Literal translation:

When I came to this country I was a poor man,
Then I bought a little chicken and began housekeeping.
If people ask the name of my little chicken,
Gickerigie is the name of my little chicken.

Then I bought a duck and began housekeeping.
If people ask the name of my little duck,
End-of-the-string is the name of my little duck

Then I bought a cow (etc)
Open-and-shut is the name of my cow (etc)

Then I bought a little goose
Bobtail is the name of my little goose.

Then I bought a horse
Oats-mouth is the name of my horse.

Then I bought a dog
Always-well is the name of my dog.

Then I bought a house
In-and-out is the name of my house.

Then I got a wife and began housekeeping.
If people ask the name of my little wife,
Hell-devil is the name of my wife,
In-and-out is the name of my house,
Always-well is the name of my dog,
Oats-mouth is the name of my horse,
Bobtail is the name of my little goose,
Open-and-shut is the name of my cow,
End-of-the-string is the name of my little duck,
Gickerigie is the name of my little chicken.

Folksinger Oscar Brand popularized this old song in the late 1950s with his own translation. Here is his version.

When I First Came to This Land

Words and music: Oscar Brand.
TRO - © Copyright 1957 (renewed), 1965 (renewed) Ludlow Music, Inc. New York, NY. Used by permission.

When I first came to this land, I was not a wealthy man.
Then I built myself a shack, I did what I could.
I called my shack, Break my back.
Still the land was sweet and good, I did what I could.

When I first came to this land, I was not a wealthy man.
Then I bought myself a cow, I did what I could.
I called my cow, No milk now.
I called my shack, Break my back.
Still the land was sweet and good, I did what I could.

When I first (etc)
Then I bought myself a horse, I did what I could.
I called my horse, Lame of course.
I called my cow, No milk now.
I called my shack, Break my back.
Still the land (etc.)

Then I bought myself a duck,
I called my duck, Out of luck.
Then I got myself a wife,
I called my wife, Joy of my life.

When I first came to this land, I was not a wealthy man.
Then I got myself a son, I did what I could.
I told my son: "My work's done."
For the land was sweet and good, I did what I could.

The Sheepstealer

Many English people came to America unwillingly, as punishment for crimes. Punishment for poaching and stealing sheep in England varied from forced service in the army or navy to death by hanging. The usual sentences, however, were seven years transportation for poaching, and fourteen years transportation for sheep-stealing. Transportation to British colonies as punishment began in the 17th century and continued throughout the 18th. After the American Revolution, English criminals were transported from Britain to New South Wales in Australia and to Van Dieman's Land (Tasmania). Despite the harsh penalties, Englishmen with hungry families continued to poach and to steal sheep.

The Pillory

The Sheepstealer

Words and music: anonymous.

I am a brisk lad, and my fortune is bad. Oh, and I am most wonderful poor. Now indeed I intend my fortune to mend, And to build a house down on the moor, my brave boys, And to build a house down on the moor.

I am a brisk lad, and my fortune is bad,
Oh, and I am most wonderful poor.
Now indeed I intend my fortune to mend,
And to build a house down on the moor, my brave boys,
And to build a house down on the moor.

I'll ride all around in another man's ground,
And I'll take a fat sheep for my own.
Oh I'll end of his life by the aid of my knife,
And then I will carry him home, my brave boys,
Oh and then I will carry him home.

My children shall pull the skin from the ewe,
And I'll go to a place where there's none.
When the constable do come, I'll stand with my gun,
And I'll swear all I have is my own, my brave boys,
And I'll swear all I have is my own.

Soldier, Soldier Will You Marry Me

All able-bodied men in the colonies were expected to take up arms when danger threatened. Soldiers in the militia were responsible for providing their own weapons, horses and clothing. A colonial soldier was likely to pick up what he could, wherever he could. "Soldier, Soldier Will You Marry Me" is an American song with English antecedents.

Soldier, Soldier Will You Marry Me

Words and music: anonymous.

Sol-dier, sol-dier will you mar-ry me, With your mus-ket, fife and drum? Oh, how can I mar-ry such a pret-ty girl as you, When I have no hat to put on? Off to the hab-er-dash-er she did go, as fast as she could run, Bought him a hat, the best that was there, And the sol-dier put it on.

Soldier, soldier will you marry me,
With your musket, fife and drum?
Oh, how can I marry such a pretty girl as you,
When I have no hat to put on?
Off to the haberdasher she did go, as fast as she could run,
Bought him a hat, the best that was there,
And the soldier put it on.

Soldier, soldier will you marry me,
With your musket, fife and drum?
Oh, how can I marry such a pretty girl as you,
When I have no coat to put on?
Off to the tailor she did go, as fast as she could run,
Bought him a coat, the best that was there,
And the soldier put it on.

Soldier, soldier will you marry me,
With your musket, fife and drum?
Oh, how can I marry such a pretty girl as you,

When I have no boots to put on?
Off to the cobbler she did go, as fast as she could run,
Bought him a pair of the best that was there,
And the soldier put them on.

Soldier, soldier will you marry me,
With your musket, fife and drum?
Oh, how can I marry such a pretty girl as you,
When I have no pants to put on?
Off to the tailor she did go, as fast as she could run,
Bought him a pair, the best that was there,
And the soldier put them on.

Now soldier, soldier will you marry me,
With your musket, fife and drum?
Well, how can I marry such a pretty girl as you,
With a wife and three kids back home?

Colonial America, 18th Century

James Edward Oglethorpe

Devil's Dream and Red-Haired Boy

In Ireland, in 1690, William of Orange defeated James II at the Boyne River, and Ireland's fortunes took a rapid turn for the worse. Irish Catholics were subjected to penal laws, denying their rights to buy land, to educate their children, to bear arms or to vote. Scots-Irish Presbyterians were also subjected to religious discrimination, although not as severe as that directed against Catholics. These conditions prompted a large migration of Irish people to America during the 18th century, as free men and as indentured servants. They brought along their songs and their instruments, including a new musical tradition that was developing in Britain and Ireland, that of transferring traditional folk melodies to the baroque violin. In America, the Irish fiddle styles dominated, and the fiddle quickly became America's favorite folk instrument.

Devil's Dream

Music: anonymous.

Red-Haired Boy

Music: anonymous.

Whiskey in the Jar

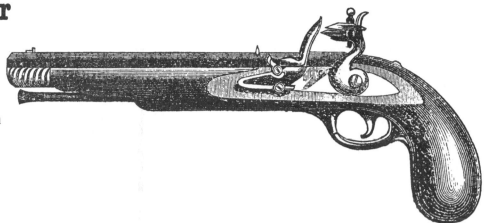

In much of colonial America, independent, self-sufficient, hard-working Americans didn't have much use for royalty or aristocracy, and they loved songs where the poor challenged the rich. The old Irish song "Whiskey in the Jar" became an American favorite.

Whiskey in the Jar

Words and music: anonymous.

As I was go-ing o-ver that far famed Ker-ry Moun-tain, I met with Cap-tain Far-rell and his mon-ey he was count-ing, I first pro-duced my pis-tol, and then pro-duced my ra-pier, Say-ing, "Stand and de-li-ver for you are my bold de-ceiv-er." Mush-a ring-um dur-um da, Whack fol the dad-dy-o Whack fol the dad-dy-o There's whis-key in the jar.

As I was going over that far famed Kerry Mountain,
I met with Captain Ferrell and his money he was counting,
I first produced my pistol, and then produced my rapier,
Saying, "Stand and deliver for you are my bold deceiver."
Musha ringum durum da,
Whack fol the daddy-o, whack fol the daddy-o,
There's whiskey in the jar.

He counted out his money and it was a pretty penny,
I put it in my pocket and I gave it to my Jennie.
She sighed and she swore that she never would betray me,
But the devil take the women for they never can be easy,
Musha ringum durum da,
Whack fol the daddy-o, whack fol the daddy-o,
There's whiskey in the jar.

I went unto my chamber, all for to take a slumber,
I dreamt of gold and jewels and for sure it was no wonder,
But Jennie drew my charges and she filled them up with water,
Then she sent for Captain Farrell to be ready for the slaughter,
Musha ringum durum da,
Whack fol the daddy-o, whack fol the daddy-o,
There's whiskey in the jar.

And 'twas early in the morning, before I rose to travel,
Up comes a band of footmen, and likewise Captain Farrell.
I then produced my pistol for she stole away my rapier,
But I couldn't shoot the water, so a prisoner I was taken.
Musha ringum durum da,
Whack fol the daddy-o, whack fol the daddy-o,
There's whiskey in the jar.

And if anyone can save me 'tis my brother in the army,
If I could learn his station, in Cork or in Killarney,
If he would come and join me we'd go rovin' in Kilkenney,
I'll engage he'd treat me fairer than me darlin', sportin' Jennie.
Musha ringum durum da,
Whack fol the daddy-o, whack fol the daddy-o,
There's whiskey in the jar.

Michael Row the Boat Ashore

By the beginning of the 18th century the complexion of the plantation worker in America was changing from white indentured servant to black slave. For the next 150 years, millions of Africans would be forcibly removed from their homes and brought to America. They came from all along the west coast of Africa, and countless villages in the interior. West Africa had entered the Iron Age well ahead of northern Europe, and by the Middle Ages there were great Moslem kingdoms - Mali, Ghana, Songhai - with craft guilds, a monetary system, and a university at Timbuctu that attracted scholars from Europe and Asia. The Africans brought a rich heritage of art, music, religion and wisdom to America, including a wealth of proverbs. West Africans say:

"Knowledge is like a garden. If it is not cultivated, it cannot be harvested."

"What the child says, he has heard at home."

"One falsehood spoils a thousand truths."

"The ruin of a nation begins in the homes of its people."

"There is no medicine to cure hatred."

Africans also brought a variety of instruments, beautiful melodies, a rich tradition of harmony singing, improvisation, falsetto, and highly sophisticated and complex rhythms.

Some of the first Africans to arrive in North America were brought to the islands off the coast of Georgia and South Carolina. The only way to get to the mainland was by boat, usually rowboat. The Africans sang songs to maintain the rhythm as they rowed.

Michael Row the Boat Ashore

Words and music: anonymous.

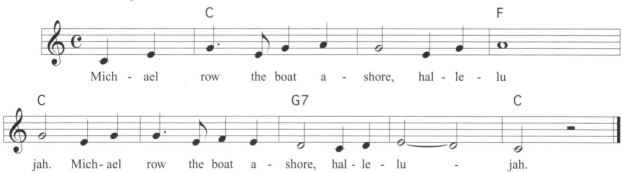

CHORUS
>Michael row the boat ashore, hallelujah,
>Michael row the boat ashore, hallelujah.

Sister help to trim the sail, hallelujah,
Sister help to trim the sail, hallelujah

CHORUS

Jordan's river is chilly and cold, hallelujah,
Chills the body but not the soul, hallelujah.

CHORUS

Michael's boat is a music boat, hallelujah,
Michael's crew is a singing crew, hallalujah.

CHORUS

Jordan's river is deep and wide, hallelujah,
I've got a home on the other side, hallelujah.

CHORUS

Jubal

On the sea islands off the coast of Georgia and South Carolina, slaves were fed in troughs, like farm animals. Survival precluded complaining to the overseer, so the African Americans sang songs in the African tradition of mask and symbol, where code words were substituted for the real words. In the chant "Jubal," the "yellow cat" is the white man. The message is: "When we kill the white man, we'll get over our troubles."

Jubal

Words and music: anonymous.

Now Ju-bal this and Ju-bal that and Ju-bal killed a yel-la cat, And get o-ver dou-ble trou-ble Ju-bal. You sift the meal, you give me the husk, You cook the bread, you give me the crust, You fry the meat, you give me the skin, And that's where my ma-ma's trou-ble be-gin. I said, Ju-bal, Ju-bal. Now Ju-bal this, and Ju-bal that, and Ju-bal killed a yel-la cat, And get o-ver dou-ble trou-ble Ju-bal.

Now Jubal this, and Jubal that, and Jubal killed a yella cat,
And get over double trouble Jubal.

You sift the meal, you give me the husk,
You cook the bread, you give me the crust,
You fry the meat, you give me the skin,
And that's where my mama's trouble begin.

I said, Jubal, Jubal.
Now Jubal this, and Jubal that, and Jubal killed a yella cat,
And get over double trouble Jubal.

Now Jubal up, and Jubal down,
And Jubal all around the town,
And Jubal ma, and Jubal pa,
And Jubal is my brother-in-law.

Now Jubal, Jubal.
Now Jubal this, and Jubal that, and Jubal killed a yella cat,
And get over double trouble Jubal.

The Mist Covered Mountain

In Scotland, the defeat of Bonnie Prince Charlie at the Battle of Culloden in 1746 resulted in the destruction of the Highland culture. The Highland Clearances began. Land-owners burned homes, destroyed farms and replaced the Highland farmers with sheep. Leaving their beloved homeland, thousands of Scots families boarded ship to the sound of the Highland bagpipes playing slow marches like "Lochaber No More" and "The Mist Covered Mountain."

Included here is a standard musical setting, plus a setting for the Highland bagpipes.

*18th Century
Highland Bagpiper*

The Mist Covered Mountain

Music: anonymous.

Bagpipe Setting

Mouth Music

Bagpipes played an important role in the lives of the Scots Highlanders. Weddings, feasts, funerals, battles and dances were performed to the accompaniment of the pipes. If a piper was not available when people wanted to dance, they re-created the sound of the pipes with their voices. They called it "mouth music."

Mouth Music

Words and music: anonymous.

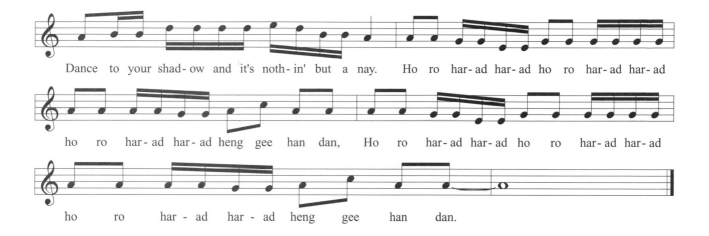

Dance to your shad-ow and it's noth-in' but a nay. Ho ro har-ad har-ad ho ro har-ad har-ad

ho ro har-ad har-ad heng gee han dan, Ho ro har-ad har-ad ho ro har-ad har-ad

ho ro har-ad har-ad heng gee han dan.

Ho ro harad harad ho ro harad harad ho ro harad harad heng gee han dan,
Ho ro harad harad ho ro harad harad ho ro harad harad heng gee han dan,
Dance to your shadow and it's good to be livin' lad,
Dance to your shadow and it's nothin' but a nay.
Dance to your shadow and it's good to be livin' lad,
Dance to your shadow and it's nothin' but a nay.

Ho ro harad harad ho ro harad harad ho ro harad harad heng gee han dan,
Ho ro harad harad ho ro harad harad ho ro harad harad heng gee han dan.
Heng heng harad harad heng heng
Harad harad heng heng harad harad heng harad harad ro,
Heng heng harad harad heng heng
Harad harad heng heng harad harad heng harad harad ro.

There are tunes in the river otter,
Pools in the river water,
Pools in the river and the river calls him.
There are tunes in the river otter,
Pools in the river water,
Pools in the river and the river calls him.

Heng heng harad harad heng heng
Harad harad heng heng harad harad heng harad harad ro.
Ho ro harad harad ho ro harad harad ho ro harad harad heng gee han dan,
Ho ro harad harad ho ro harad harad ho ro harad harad heng gee han dan.

Dance to your shadow and it's good to be livin' lad,
Dance to your shadow and it's nothin' but a nay.
Dance to your shadow and it's good to be livin' lad,
Dance to you shadow and it's nothin' but a nay.
Ho ro harad harad ho ro harad harad ho ro harad harad heng gee han dan,
Ho ro harad harad ho ro harad harad ho ro harad harad heng gee han dan.

The Hoosier

The Scots brought both their pipes and their mouth music to the New World. In addition to their voices, English, Irish and Scots Americans re-created the sound of the bagpipes with fiddles and other musical instruments. The people in the Appalachian Mountains created a stringed instrument called a dulcimer, which reproduced the sound of the pipes. On the Appalachian dulcimer, one string played the melody like the chanter on the pipes, while the other two sounded the drone.

Appalachian Dulcimer

The Hoosier

Music: anonymous.

The Greenland Whale Fishery

Much of the wealth of New England came from the sea. Massachusetts was the ship building center, and by the end of the Colonial period, about one third of all Britain's merchant ships had been built in America. American ships and seamen were among the best in the world. Specific areas in New England became identified with their own specialties: Boston and Salem with merchant voyages; Gloucester and Cape Ann with fishing; Maine with coasting (trading up and down the coast from port to port); Rhode Island with slaving; Newburyport with sugar and rum; and Southern Massachusetts with whaling. In the earliest days, whaling was done from the beach as the Indians had done for centuries. As whales became scarce, the whalemen took short voyages to sea. The English and Dutch were hunting whales in Greenland by the early 16th century, and Americans continued to hunt the area during the Colonial period. Finally, ships began to go around Cape Horn to the Pacific, and the trips lasted from one to as many as four years. Songs were important to the whalemen. With poor food, hard and dangerous work, sometimes cruel and brutal treatment, and thousands of miles between their ships and home, singing was one of the few pleasures open to the sailors. Many versions of this fo'c'sle song have been collected – from ships' logs, journals, and the merchant marine, in addition to the sailors on the whaling ships.

The Greenland Whale Fishery

Words and music: anonymous.

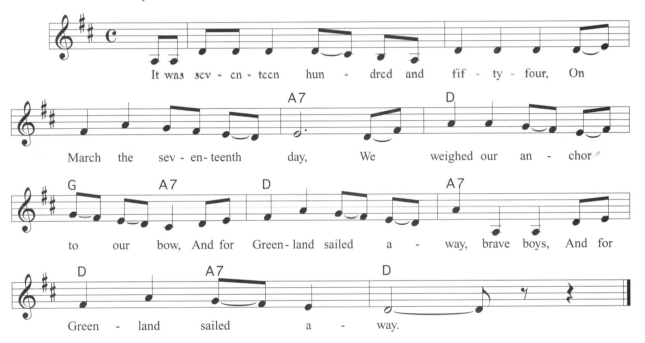

It was seventeen hundred and fifty-four,
On March the seventeenth day,
We weighed our anchor to our bow,
And for Greenland sailed away, brave boys,
And for Greenland sailed away.

The lookout in the crosstree stood,
With his spyglass in his hand,
"There's a whale, there's a whale, there's a whalefish," he cried,
"And she blows at every span, brave boys,
And she blows at every span."

Now the boats were launched, and the men aboard,
And the whale was in full view.
Resolved was each seaman bold,
To steer where the whalefish blew, brave boys,
To steer where the whalefish blew.

We struck that whale and the line paid out,
And he gave one slap with his tail,
We lost that boat and five good men
And we never caught that whale, brave boys,
And we never caught that whale.

"Bad news, bad news," our captain he cried,
"For it grieves my heart full sore."
But the losing of that hundred barrel whale,
It grieved him ten times more, brave boys,
It grieved him ten times more.

Oh, Greenland is a dreadful place,
A land that's never green,
Where there's ice and snow, and the whalefishes blow,
And the daylight's seldom seen, brave boys,
And the daylight's seldom seen.

The Death of General Wolfe

The Indian balance of power was disrupted when the Europeans arrived on the East Coast. New alliances between tribes were formed, and also alliances with the French and English. During the French and Indian Wars, the Algonquians formed an alliance with the French, and the Iroquois federation allied with the British. The powerful Iroquois tilted the scales in Britain's favor.

The decisive battle of the French and Indian Wars was the Battle of Quebec, which took place on the Plains of Abraham near Quebec City. On a cloudy night in September 1759, British forces, under the leadership of popular young British General James Wolfe, climbed the steep cliffs, and overpowered a small French force. By 8:00 a.m. the British forces were on the Plains of Abraham ready to fight. However, they waited until Montcalm's forces were lined up and prepared before they opened fire, around 10:00 a.m. The Battle claimed the lives of both Wolfe and Montcalm. Wolfe died just after news came that victory was at hand. Montcalm died the next day. A ballad, called "The Death of General Wolfe," was printed on a broadsheet, and sold thousands of copies in the American colonies.

The Death of General Wolfe

Words and music: anonymous.

Come all ye young men all, let this delight you, Cheer up ye young men all, let noth - ing
fright you, Ne - ver let your cour - age fail when you're brought to
tri - al, Nor let your fan - cy move at the first de - ni - al.

Come all ye young men all, let this delight you,
Cheer up ye young men all, let nothing fright you,
Never let your courage fail when you're brought to trial,
Nor let your fancy move at the first denial.

So then this gallant youth did cross the ocean,
To free America from her invasion,
He landed at Quebec with all his party,
The city to attack, being brave and hearty.

The French drew up their men, for death prepared.
In one another's face the armies stared,
While Wolfe and Montcalm together walked,
Between their armies they like brothers talked.

Each man then took his post at their retire,
So then these numerous hosts began to fire,
The cannon on each side did roar like thunder,
And youths in all their pride were torn asunder.

The drums did loudly beat, colors were flying,
The purple gore did stream and men lay dying,
When shot off from his horse fell this brave hero,
And we lament his loss in weeds of sorrow.

The French began to break, their ranks were flying,
Wolfe seemed to revive while he lay dying,
He lifted up his head as drums did rattle,
And to his army said, "How goes the battle?"

His aide-de-camp replied, " 'Tis in our favor,
Quebec, with all her pride, nothing can save her,
She falls into our hands with all her treasure."
"Oh then," brave Wolfe replied, "I die with pleasure."

The American Revolution

The British Grenadiers

This ever-popular British tune dates back to the 16th century.
The words date from the late 17th or early 18th century.

The British Grenadiers

Words and music: anonymous.

Some talk of Al ex an der, and some of Her cu les, Of Hec - tor and Ly - san - der, and such great names as these, But of all the world's great he - roes, there's none that can com - pare, With a tow row row, with a tow row row, to the Brit - ish Gren - a - diers.

Some talk of Alexander, and some of Hercules,
Of Hector and Lysander, and such great names as these,
But of all the world's great heroes, there's none that can compare,
With a tow row row, with a tow row row, to the British Grenadiers.

None of those ancient heroes e'er saw a cannon ball,
Or knew the force of powder to slay their foes withal,
But our brave boys do know it, and banish all their fears,
Singing, "Tow row row, with a tow row row, to the British Grenadiers."

When e'er we are commanded to storm the palisades,
Our leaders march with fusees, and we with hand grenades,
We throw them from the glacis about our enemies ears,
Singing, "Tow row row, with a tow row row, to the British Grenadiers."

And when the siege is over, we to the town repair,
The townsmen cry, "Harrah, boys, here comes a Grenadier.
Here come the Grenadiers, my boys, who know no doubts or fears,"
Singing, "Tow row row, with a tow row row, to the British Grenadiers."

Then let us fill a bumper, and drink a health to those
Who carry caps and pouches, and wear the looped clothes,
May they and their commanders live happy all their years!
With a tow row row, with a tow row row, to the British Grenadiers.

Free America

The American colonists viewed the presence of British troops in America with favor, as long as the threat of French or Indian attack remained. After the French and Indian Wars, however, the Americans saw no need for continued British military presence. On the other hand, from the British point of view, the need was increasing. The newly gained territory needed protection, there was no organized government west of the Allegheny Mountains, and the British wanted the Americans to share in the increased cost of governing the colonies.

The British closed the west to settlement, levied taxes and duties, enforced the collection of these taxes, and stationed troops in New York and Boston. The presence of these troops was distasteful to the Americans, who were more interested in freedom than in independence from England. In 1770, Dr. Joseph Warren, who was later killed at Bunker Hill, wrote the song "Free America" to the tune of "The British Grenadiers." On two separate occasions, Dr. Warren delivered orations against the Boston Massacre, one of them in the presence of, and in defiance of, British soldiers. Dr. Warren also sent Paul Revere on his famous ride.

Free America

Words: Dr. Joseph Warren. Music: anonymous.

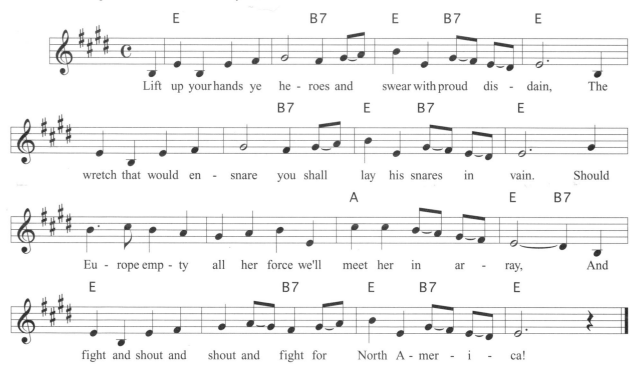

Lift up your hands ye heroes and swear with proud disdain,
The wretch that would ensnare you shall lay his snares in vain.
Should Europe empty all her force we'll meet her in array,
And fight and shout and shout and fight for North America!

We led fair Franklin hither, and lo, the desert smiled,
A paradise of pleasure was opened to the world.
Your harvest, bold Americans, no power shall snatch away,
Huzzah, huzzah, huzzah, huzzah, for free America!

Torn from a world of tyrants beneath this western sky,
We formed a new dominion, a land of liberty.
The world shall own we're masters here, then hasten on the day,
Huzzah, huzzah, huzzah, huzzah, for free America!

Some future day shall crown us the masters of the main.
Our fleets shall speak in thunder, to England, France and Spain,
And the nations o'er the oceans' spread shall tremble and obey,
The sons, the sons, the sons, the sons of brave America!

Castle Island Song

Tension between British soldiers and Boston civilians increased. An incident, in which some small boys threw snowballs at a sentry, escalated into an angry mob. British troops fired on the citizens, killing three and wounding eight. After the Boston Massacre, as the incident was called, British troops were confined to quarters on Castle Island, where they sang this song, written to the traditional English melody "Down, Derry Down." "The Castle Island Song" was popular among American Royalists.

Castle Island Song

Words and music: anonymous.

You simple Bostonians I'd have you beware,
Of your Liberty Tree I would have you take care,
For if that we chance to return to the town,
Your houses and stores will come tumbling down,
Derry down, down, down, derry down.

If you'll not agree to Old England's laws,
I fear that King Hancock will soon get the yaws,
But he need not fear, for I swear we will,
For the want of a doctor give him a hard pill.
Derry down, down, down, derry down.

A brave reinforcement we soon think to get,
Then we will make you poor pumpkins to sweat,
Our drums they will rattle and then you will run,
To the devil himself, from the sight of a gun,
Derry down, down, down, derry down.

Our fleet and our army they soon will arrive,
Then to a bleak island you shall not us drive,
In every house you shall have three or four,
And if that does not please you, you'll have half a score,
Derry down, down, down, derry down,
Derry down, down, down, derry down.

The Rich Lady Over the Sea

As British taxes increased, so did colonial resistance. Colonists resented the Sugar Act and the Currency Act, both passed in 1764. The Sons of Liberty rioted in the streets of Boston to protest passage of the Stamp Act in 1765. The Revenue Act of 1767 further inflamed the colonists. The Tea Act of 1773, which made it possible for the British East India Company to sell its tea in America at prices well below those of American tea merchants, inspired angry colonists to throw British East India tea into Boston Harbor. Similar "tea parties" took place up and down the coast.

The Rich Lady Over the Sea

Words and music: anonymous.

There was a rich la-dy lived o-ver the sea, And she was an is-land queen. Her daugh-ter lived off in the new coun-try, With an o-cean of wa-ter be-tween. With an o-cean of wa-ter be-tween, With an o-cean of wa-ter be-tween.

There was a rich lady lived over the sea,
And she was an island queen.
Her daughter lived off in the new country,
With an ocean of water between.
With an ocean of water between,
With an ocean of water between.

The old lady's pockets were filled with gold,
Yet never contented was she,
So she ordered her daughter to pay her a tax
Of thruppence a pound on the tea.
Of thruppence a pound on the tea,
Of thruppence a pound on the tea.

"Oh mother, dear mother," the daughter replied,
"I'll not do the thing that you ask,
I'm willing to pay a fair price on the tea,
But never the thruppenney tax." (etc)

"You shall!" cried the mother, and reddened with rage,
"For you're my own daughter, you see,
And it's only proper that daughter should pay
Her mother a tax on the tea." (etc)

She ordered her servant to come up to her,
And to wrap up a package of tea,
And eager for thruppence a pound she put in
Enough for a large family. (etc)

The tea was conveyed to her daughter's own door,
All down by the oceanside,
But the bouncing girl poured out every pound
On the dark and the boiling tide. (etc)

And then she called out to the island queen,
"Oh mother, dear mother," called she,
"Your tea you may have when 'tis steeped enough,
But never a tax from me!" (etc)

The Boston Massacre

Yankee Doodle

"Yankee Doodle" was one of the favorite songs of the American Revolution. Theories about the origins of the melody vary. Some say it was popular in Holland around 1500. Others say it came from Southern Europe in the Middle Ages, or from Germany, France, Hungary, Persia, Biscay, Wales, Ireland or England. It was reportedly sung by Charles I's Cavaliers ridiculing Cromwell's Roundheads.

Many scholars attribute the original British words to Dr. Richard S. Schuckberg, a British army surgeon. Dr. Schuckberg reportedly wrote the words in the 1740s or early 1750s, ridiculing the colonial American soldiers. It became popular among British soldiers during the French and Indian Wars. The earliest known publication of "Yankee Doodle" is believed to have been in the New York Journal on October 12, 1768.

As hostilities between British and American soldiers began, British soldiers sang:

Yankee Doodle came to town,
For to buy a firelock,
We will tar and feather him,
And so we will John Hancock.

American soldiers adopted Yankee Doodle as their own, and sang it as the British retreated from Concord and Lexington. They also made up verses making fun of their own officers, including General Washington.

British caricature of American militiaman

Yankee Doodle

Words and music: anonymous.

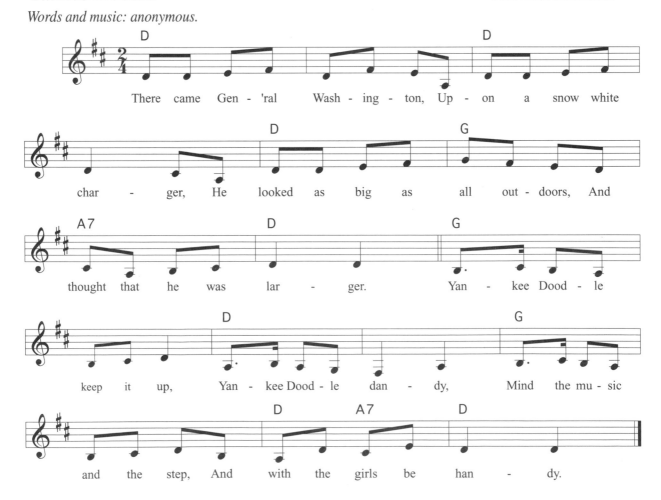

There came Gen-'ral Wash-ing-ton, Up-on a snow white charger, He looked as big as all out-doors, And thought that he was lar-ger. Yan-kee Dood-le keep it up, Yan-kee Dood-le dan-dy, Mind the mu-sic and the step, And with the girls be han-dy.

Father and I went down to camp
Along with Captain Goodwin,
And there we saw the men and boys
As thick as hasty puddin'

CHORUS

> Yankee Doodle keep it up,
> Yankee Doodle dandy,
> Mind the music and the step,
> And with the girls be handy.

And then the feathers on his hat
They looked so 'tarnal fincy,
I wanted peskily to get,
To give to my Jemimy.

CHORUS

And there we saw a thousand men,
As rich as Squire David,
And what they wasted every day
I wish it could be saved.

CHORUS

And there they'd fife away like fun,
And play on corn stalk fiddles,
And some had ribbons red as blood
All bound around their middles.

CHORUS

Uncle Sam came there to change
Some pancakes and some onions,
For molasses cakes to carry home
To give his wife and young 'uns.

CHORUS

And there they had a swamping gun
As large as a log of maple,
Upon a deuced little cart,
A load for father's cattle.

CHORUS

And every time they'd shoot it off
It took a horn of powder,
It made a noise like father's gun,
Only a nation louder.

CHORUS

And there was Captain Washington,
With gentlefolks about him,
They say he's grown so 'tarnal proud
He will not ride without them.

CHORUS

And there was Captain Washington,
Upon a strapping stallion,
And giving orders to his men,
I guess there was a million.

CHORUS

There came General Washington,
Upon a snow white charger,
He looked as big as all outdoors,
And thought that he was larger.

CHORUS

Yankee Doodle is the tune
Americans delight in,
'Twill do to whistle, sing or play,
And is just the thing for fighting.

CHORUS

The Battle of the Kegs

The best parody of Yankee Doodle was "The Battle of the Kegs," written by Francis Hopkinson, American statesman, artist and poet. Hopkinson, a signer of the Declaration of Independence, designed the Great Seal of New Jersey, claimed to have designed the American flag, wrote a number of patriotic poems and songs, and his "Seven Songs" is said to be the first book of music published by an American composer.

"The Battle of the Kegs" was inspired by an incident whereupon the Americans filled some kegs with powder, primed them to explode on contact, and set them afloat. To the amusement of the colonists, the British fired on the kegs to explode them. The American press had fun with the incident, too. On January 21, 1778, the New Jersey Gazette reported the story. Here are some excerpts:

"Yesterday... several kegs... made their appearance. An alarm was immediately spread through the city; various reports prevailed, filling the city and the royal troops with consternation. Some reported that the kegs were filled with armed rebels who were to issue forth in the dead of night and take the city by surprise, just as the Grecians of old did from their wooden horse at the siege of Troy...

"Be this as it may,... the battle began, and it was surprising to behold the incessant blaze that was kept up against the enemy, the kegs. Both officers and men exhibited the most unparalleled skill and bravery on the occasion, whilst the citizens stood gazing as solemn witnesses of their prowess. From the *Roebuck*, and other ships of war, whole broadsides were poured into the Delaware. In short, not a wandering ship, stick or driftlog but felt the vigor of the British arms.

"The action began about sunrise, and would have been completed with great success by noon, had not an old market woman, coming down the river with provisions, let a small keg of butter fall overboard, which... floated down to the scene of action. At sight of this unexpected reinforcement of the enemy, the battle was renewed with fresh fury, and the firing was incessant 'til the evening closed the affair..."

The Battle of the Kegs

Words: Francis Hopkinson.   Music: anonymous.

'Twas ear - ly day as po - ets say, Just when the sun was ris - ing, A sol - dier stood on a log of wood And saw a sight sur - pris - ing. A sail - or too in jer - kin blue This strange ap - pear - ance view ing, First damned his eyes in great sur- prise, Then said, "Some mis - chief's brew - ing."

'Twas early day as poets say,
Just when the sun was rising,
A soldier stood on a log of wood
And saw a sight surprising.
A sailor too in jerkin blue
This strange appearance viewing,
First damned his eyes in great surprise,
Then said, "Some mischief's brewing."

"These kegs now hold the rebels bold,
Packed up like pickled herring,
And they're come down to attack the town
In this new way of ferrying.
Therefore prepare for bloody war,
These kegs must all be routed,
Or surely we despised shall be,
And British courage doubted."

Now up and down throughout the town
Most frantic scenes were acted,
And some ran here and some ran there
Like men almost distracted
Some, "fire!" cried, which some denied,
But said the earth had quaked,
And girls and boys with hideous noise
Ran through the town half naked.

The rebel vales, the rebel dales,
With rebel trees surrounded,
The distant woods, the hills and floods,
With rebel echoes sounded.
The fish below swam to and fro,
Attacked from every quarter,
"Why, sure," thought they, "the devil's to pay
Amongst folks above the water."

The cannon roar from shore to shore,
The small arms make a rattle,
Since wars began I'm sure no man
Ere saw so strange a battle.
These kegs 'tis said, though strongly made
Of rebel staves and hoops, sir,
Could not oppose their powerful foes,
The conquering British troops, sir!

A hundred men, with each a pen,
Or more, upon my words, sirs,
It is most true, would be too few
Their valor to record, sirs.
Such feats did they perform that day
Upon those wicked kegs, sirs,
That years to come, if they get home,
They'll make their boasts and brags, sirs.

Chester

Even more popular than "Yankee Doodle" was the song "Chester," written by William Billings, America's first composer of sacred music. Billings was a tanner who wrote and taught music as an avocation. His songs are still popular among choral groups, especially "Chester," "The Rose of Sharon," and "David's Lamentation." "Chester" became the anthem of the Continental Army.

Chester

Words and music: William Billings.

Let ty-rants shake their i - ron rods,
And slav-ry clank her gal ling chains,
We fear them not, we trust in God.
New Eng-land's God for - ev - er reigns.

Let tyrants shake their iron rods,
And slav'ry clank her galling chains,
We fear them not, we trust in God.
New England's God forever reigns.

The foe comes on with haughty stride,
Our troops advance with martial noise,
There veterans flee before our youth,
And generals yield to beardless boys.

What grateful offerings shall we bring,
What shall we render to the Lord?
Loud hallelujahs let us sing
And praise His name on every chord.

Johnny Has Gone for a Soldier

Nearly half the soldiers in Washington's army were of Irish origin or descent, and many songs of the Revolution were Irish. The Irish song from which the popular "Johnny Has Gone for a Soldier" originated, was called "Siubhail A Gradh," and dates back to the mid-17th century.

Irish-American soldiers sang "Johnny Has Gone for a Soldier" during both the Revolutionary War and the Civil War. Many of the soldiers sang the chorus in the original Gaelic. The Gaelic chorus (written here phonetically) translates, "Come, my love, quickly and softly we'll slip away."

Johnny Has Gone for a Soldier

Words and music: anonymous.

Valley Forge

Oh I wish I were on yon green hill, There I'd sit and cry my fill. And ev-ry tear would turn a mill, For my John-ny has gone for a sol-dier.

Shule shule shule a-roon, Shule ga sic-cir a-gus shule go kewn,

Shule ga laas og-gus sell lee-den doon, Iss ga day - thoo a-voor-neen shlawn.

Oh I wish I were on yon green hill,
There I'd sit and cry my fill.
And every tear would turn a mill,
For my Johnny has gone for a soldier.

CHORUS
    Shule, shule, shule aroon,
    Shule ga siccir agus shule go kewn,
    Shule ga laas oggus sell leeden doon,
    Iss ga day thoo avoorneen shlawn.

I'll sell my clock, I'll sell my reel,
I'll sell my only spinning wheel,
To buy my love a sword of steel,
My Johnny has gone for a soldier.

CHORUS

I'll dye my petticoat, I'll dye it red,
And round the world I will bake my bread,
Till I find my love alive or dead.
My Johnny has gone for a soldier.

CHORUS

The World Turned Upside Down

In September of 1781, while the French fleet held off the British fleet, General Washington closed in on the British troops at Yorktown. With his supplies cut off, and his escape by sea impossible, Cornwallis surrendered. The afternoon of the surrender, the British band played "The World Turned Upside Down." In the song, the mother represents England, and the daughter represents America. The would-be peacemaker farmer Pitt is William Pitt, who was head of the British ministry during the period. The tune is the old English folk melody "Down, Derry Down."

Surrender at Yorktown

The World Turned Upside Down

Words and music: anonymous.

Good-y Bull and her daugh-ter to-geth-er fell out, Both squab-bled and wran-gled and made a great rout. But the cause of the quar-rel re-mains to be told, Then lend both your ears and a tale I'll un-fold. Der-ry down, down, hey der-ry down. Then lend both your ears and a tale I'll un-fold.

Goody Bull and her daughter together fell out,
Both squabbled and wrangled and made a great rout.
But the cause of the quarrel remains to be told,
Then lend both your ears and a tale I'll unfold.
Derry down, down, hey derry down.
Then lend both your ears and a tale I'll unfold.

The old lady, it seems, took a freak in her head,
That her daughter, grown woman, might earn her own bread,
Self-applauding her scheme, she was ready to dance,
But we're often too sanguine in what we advance.
Derry down, down, hey derry down.
But we're often too sanguine in what we advance.

For mark the event, thus for fortune we're crossed,
Nor should people reckon without their good host,
The daughter was sulky and wouldn't come to,
And pray what in this case could the old woman do?
Derry down, down, hey derry down.
And pray what in this case could the old woman do?

"Zounds, neighbor," quoth Pitt, "what the devil's the matter?
A man cannot rest in his home for your clatter."
"Alas," cries the daughter, "Here's dainty fine work,
The old woman grows harder than Jew or than Turk.
Derry down, down, hey derry down.
The old woman grows harder than Jew or than Turk."

"She be damned!" says the farmer, and to her he goes,
First roars in her ears, then tweaks her old nose,
"Hello Goody, what ails you? Wake, woman, I say,
I am come to make peace in this desperate fray,
Derry down, down, hey derry down,
I am come to make peace in this desperate fray."

"Alas," cries the old woman, "And must I comply?
But I'd rather submit than the hussy should die."
"Pooh, prithee, be quiet, be friends and agree,
You must surely be right if you're guided by me,
Derry down, down, hey derry down,
You must surely be right if you're guided by me."

Hail Columbia

The Revolutionary War ended officially with the Treaty of Paris on April 19, 1783, and thirteen of the thirty-three British colonies in the Americas became an independent nation. A number of patriotic songs were written to commemorate the creation of the new nation, including "Hail Columbia." Joseph Hopkinson, son of Francis Hopkinson, wrote the words in 1798 to help raise the national cause above factional differences. Hopkinson's words were set to the tune of Philip Phile's "The President's March," and "Hail Columbia" quickly became a national favorite.

Hail Columbia

Words: Joseph Hopkinson. Music: Philip Phile.

Hail Co - lum - bia hap - py land, Hail ye he - roes heaven born band, Who fought and bled in free - dom's - cause, Who fought and bled in free - dom's - cause. And when the storm of war is gone, En - joyed the peace your val - or won. Let in - de - pen - dence be your boast, Ev - er mind - ful what it costs, Ev - er grate - ful for the prize. Let its al - tar reach the skies. Firm, u - nit - ed let us be, Ral - lying round our lib - er - ty, As a band of bro - thers joined, Peace and safe - ty we shall find.

Hail Columbia happy land,
Hail ye heroes heaven born band,
Who fought and bled in freedom's cause,
Who fought and bled in freedom's cause,
And when the storm of war is gone,
Enjoyed the peace your valor won.
Let independence be your boast,
Ever mindful what it costs,
Ever grateful for the prize.
Let its altar reach the skies.

CHORUS

       Firm, united let us be,
       Rallying round our liberty,
       As a band of brothers joined,
       Peace and safety we shall find.

Immortal patriots rise once more,
Defend your rights, defend your shore,
Let no rude foe with impious hand,
Let no rude foe with impious hand,
Invade the shrine where sacred lies
Of toil and blood the well-earned prize.
While offering peace, sincere and just,
In heaven we place a manly trust,
That truth and justice will prevail,
And every scheme of bondage fail.

CHORUS

Sound, sound the trump of fame,
Let Washington's great name
Ring through the world with loud applause,
Ring through the world with loud applause.
Let every clime to freedom dear
Listen with a joyful ear,
With equal skill, with godlike power,
He governs in the fearful hour
Of horrid war, or guides with ease
The happier times of honest peace.

CHORUS

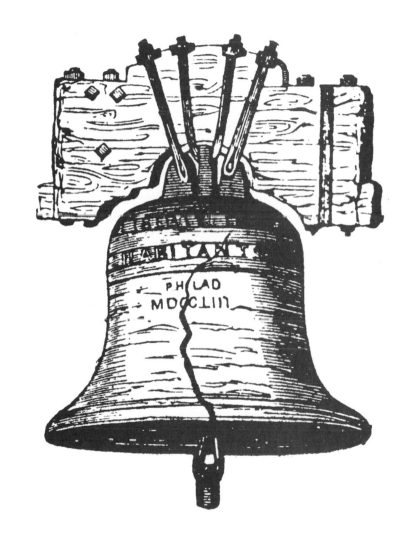

The War of 1812

The Eighth of January

This American fiddle tune was written to commemorate the Battle of New Orleans, which took place on the eighth of January, 1815.

The Eighth of January

Music: anonymous.

Sinclair's Defeat

In the years between the American Revolution and the War of 1812 a number of battles were fought between the United States and the Indian nations in the Northwest Territory. In 1791, Chief Little Turtle defeated Arthur St. Claire's army in Indiana Territory. The song "Sinclair's Defeat" was written by one of his soldiers.

General Arthur St. Clair

Sinclair's Defeat

Words and music: anonymous.

To mention our brave officers is what I write to do,
No sons of Mars e'er fought more brave or with more courage true.
To Captain Bradfort I belonged, in his artillery,
He fell that day among the slain, a valiant man was he.

To mention our brave officers is what I write to do,
No sons of Mars e'er fought more brave or with more courage true.
To Captain Bradfort I belonged, in his artillery,
He fell that day among the slain, a valiant man was he.

Parliament of England

Many Americans were convinced that the British were supporting the Indian resistance, and when they found British guns on the battlefield after the Battle of Tippecanoe, they began openly advocating driving the British from Canada. Britain and France continued to wage war against each other, and the United States was profiting greatly as American ships carried goods to both countries. Then both the British and French set up blockades, and the profits ceased. Tensions increased when British ships began stopping American ships on the high seas, searching for British deserters, and sometimes impressing American seamen into British service. These tensions, plus the desire for territorial expansion on the part of Southerners and Westerners, led to a declaration of war against Britain on June 18, 1812. "Parliament of England" was originally a navy song, but it quickly became popular among the militia as well.

Parliament of England

Words and music: anonymous.

You par-lia-ment of Eng-land, you lords and com-mons too, Con-sid-er well what you're a-bout and what you mean to do. You're now at war with Yan-kees, I'm sure you'll rue the day You roused the Sons of Lib-er-ty in North A-mer-i-ca.

You parliament of England, you lords and commons too,
Consider well what you're about and what you mean to do.
You're now at war with Yankees, I'm sure you'll rue the day
You roused the Sons of Liberty in North America.

You first confined our commerce, you said our ships shan't trade,
You then impressed our seamen and used them as your slaves,
You then insulted Rodgers while cruising on the main,
And had we not declared war, you'd have done it o'er again.

Remember, you Britons, far distant is the day
That e'er you'll gain by British force your lost America,
Go tell your king and parliament, by all the world it's known,
That British force by sea and land's by Yankees overthrown.

You thought our frigates were but few, and Yankees could not fight,
Until bold Hull the *Guerrière* took, and banished her from sight.
The *Wasp* next took your *Frolic*, you nothing said to that,
The *Poictiers* being off the coast, of course you took her back.

Next your *Macedonian*, no finer ship could swim,
Decatur took her gilt-work off, and then he took her in.
The *Java* by a Yankee ship was sunk, you all must know,
The *Peacock*, in all her pride, by Lawrence down did go.

Then upon Lake Erie brave Perry had some fun,
You own he beat your naval force and caused them all to run,
While Chauncey on Ontario, the like ne'er known before,
Your British squadron beat complete, some took, some run ashore.

Then your brave Indian allies, you called them by that name,
Until they turned the tomahawk, they "savages" became,
Your mean insinuations they despised from their souls,
And joined the Sons of Liberty that scorn to be controlled.

Remember, you Britons, far distant is the day
That e'er you'll gain by British force your lost America,
Go tell you king and parliament, by all the world it's known,
That British force by sea and land's by Yankees overthrown.

Grant us free trade and commerce, don't you impress our men,
Give up all claims to Canada, then we'll make peace again.
Then England, we'll respect you, and treat you as a friend,
Respect our flag and citizens, then all these wars will end.

The Noble Lads of Canada

The land war went poorly for the United States. In 1812 U.S. forces invaded Canada across the Detroit River. Canadian forces drove the Americans back, capturing Detroit and General Hull's army. American soldiers crossed the Niagara and occupied Queenstown Heights, but when the New York militia refused to cross the Canadian border to help, they were defeated too. The Canadians sang "The Noble Lads of Canada." After the Battle of Plattsburg, an American version of "The Noble Lads of Canada" was printed on a broadside, telling the story of the defeat of the Canadians by Macdonough on Lake Champlain. This is the Canadian version.

The Noble Lads of Canada

Words and music: anonymous.

Come all you British heroes, I pray you lend your ears,
Draw up your British forces, and then your volunteers,
We're going to fight the Yankee boys by water and by land,
And we never will return, till we conquer sword in hand,
We're the noble lads of Canada, come to arms, boys, come!

Oh, now the time has come, my boys, to cross the Yankees' line,
Remember they were rebels once, and conquered John Burgoyne,
We'll subdue those haughty democrats, and pull their dwellings down,
And we'll have the states inhabited with subjects to the crown,
We're the noble lads of Canada, come to arms, boys, come!

The Constitution and the Guerrière

The war at sea was definitely one-sided. Britannia ruled the waves. The British navy had nearly a thousand fighting ships, the American navy had seventeen. However, two American naval victories on lakes helped shape the course of the war. Master-Commandant Perry defeated the British ships on Lake Erie, and Master-Commandant Macdonough did the same on Lake Champlain. On the high seas,

American navy vessels and privateers harassed British shipping, and on a one-to-one basis gained some notable victories, including that of the *USS Constitution* ("Old Ironsides") over the *HMS Guerrière*. This broadside ballad was set to the tune of the English drinking song "A Drop of Brandy-o," and gained wide popularity among American sailors.

The Constitution and the Guerrière

Words and music: anonymous.

Oft times it has been told how the British seamen bold, Could flog the tars of France so neat and handy-o, And they never found their match, till the Yankees did them catch, Oh the Yankee boys for fighting are the dandy-o!

Oft times it has been told how the British seamen bold,
Could flog the tars of France so neat and handy-o,
And they never found their match, till the Yankees did them catch,
Oh the Yankee boys for fighting are the dandy-o.

The *Guerrière* a frigate bold on the foamy ocean rolled,
Commanded by proud Dacres, the Grandee-o,
With as choice a British crew as a rammer ever drew,
They could flog the tars of France so neat and handy-o.

This boasting Briton cries, "Make that Yankee ship your prize,
You can in thirty minutes do it handy-o,
Or in twenty-five I'm sure and if you do it in a score,
I'll give to you a double share of brandy-o."

When the *Constitution* hove in view, says proud Dacres to his crew,
"Come clear the ship for action and be handy-o!"
Now the British shot blew hot, which the Yankees answered not,
Till they got within the distance they called handy-o.

The first broadside we poured swept their mainmast overboard,
Which made their lofty frigate look abandoned-o.
Our second told so well that their fore and mizzen fell,
Which downed the royal ensign neat and handy-o.

Then proud Dacres came on board to deliver up his sword,
Said, "I did not think the Yankees were so handy-o."
"Oh, keep your sword," says Hull, "if it only makes you dull,
Cheer up and let us have a little brandy-o."

To Anacreon in Heaven

While the French and Indian Wars had diminished Indian power in the Northeast, the final stand against white encroachment was made when Shawnee Chief Tecumseh joined with the British in the War of 1812, and was commissioned a Brigadier General commanding 2,000 Indian troops. Here is an excerpt from a speech by Tecumseh to the Creek Nation, inviting them to join with him and the British against the Americans:

"Why not vanquish the Americans and free ourselves from their yoke, their schools, their spinning wheels, their plows and clothing, these emblems of our subjugation and disgrace, these fetters of our freedom. The British do not try to make us forget the God of our fathers. They do not wish to make us live in the houses of the white men, that we may hew their wood and draw their water. They will neither change our customs nor drive us from our homes. The Americans we must fight, not the British. The Americans are our eternal foes, the hungry devourers of the country of our fathers."

Tecumseh was killed at the Battle of Moravian Town in 1813. The following year, a British fleet, carrying General Ross's army, entered Chesapeake Bay. They occupied Washington, D.C. but were driven back at Baltimore. Francis Scott Key, attempting to secure the release of a friend, was held on board a British warship in Chesapeake Bay while the ship bombarded Fort McHenry. When the bombardment ended, and the American flag was still flying, Key penned the verse to "The Defense of Fort McHenry," later re-titled "The Star Spangled Banner." Key's brother-in-law suggested he use a tune currently popular in America called "To Anacreon in Heaven." It had been the theme song of the Anacreontic Club in London, an exclusive organization of wealthy London men who gathered together for music, food and drink. The Anacreontic Club took its name from the Greek poet Anacreon, whose poems celebrated Venus, the goddess of love, and Bacchus, the god of wine. First published in England around 1780, the English song's popularity in the United States inspired other Americans, including Robert Treat Paine, Jr., son of Robert Treat Paine, signer of the Declaration of Independence, to write patriotic songs using the same tune.

Chief Tecumseh

To Anacreon in Heaven

Words: Ralph Tomlinson. Music: John Stafford Smith.

To Anacreon in heaven where he sat in full glee,
A few sons of harmony sent a petition,
That he their inspirer and patron would be,
When this answer arrived from the jolly old Grecian:
"Voice, fiddle and flute, no longer be mute,
I'll lend you my name and inspire you to boot!
And besides I'll instruct you like me to entwine
The myrtle of Venus and Bacchus's vine."

The news through Olympus immediately flew,
When old Thunder pretended to give himself airs,
"If these mortals are suffered their scheme to pursue,
The devil a goddess will stay above stairs,
Hark! already they cry, in transports of joy,
A fig for Parnassus, to Rowley's we'll fly,
And there my good fellows, we'll learn to entwine
The myrtle of Venus with Bacchus's vine."

"The yellow-haired god, and his nine fusty maids,
To the hill of old Lud will incontinent flee,
Idalia will boast but of tenantless shades,
And the biforked hill a mere desert will be,
My thunder, no fear on't, will soon do its errand,
And, damn me I'll swinge the ringleaders, I warrant
I'll trim the young dogs, for thus daring to twine
The myrtle of Venus with Bacchus's vine."

Apollo rose up and said, "Prythee ne'er quarrel,
Good king of the gods, with my votaries below
Your thunder is useless" - then showing his laurel,
Cried, "Sic evitabile fulmen, you know!
Then over each head my laurels I'll spread,
So my sons from your crackers no mischief shall dread,
Whilst snug in their club-room, they jovially twine
The myrtle of Venus with Bacchus's vine."

Patriotic Diggers

The presence of the British fleet in Chesapeake Bay aroused the people in Philadelphia. Local citizens of all walks of life volunteered their labors to improve fortifications of the city. Printer and poet Samuel Woodworth, who is best known for his song "The Old Oaken Bucket," wrote the words to this song.

Patriotic Diggers

Words: Samuel Woodworth. Music: anonymous.

John-ny Bull be-ware, keep at your prop-er dis-tance, Else we'll make you stare at our firm re-sist-ance, Let a-lone the lads who are free-dom tast-ing, Rec-ol-lect our dads gave you once a bast-ing. Pick-axe, shov-el, spade, crow-bar, hoe and bar-row, Bet-ter not in-vade, Yan-kees have the mar-row!

Johnny Bull beware, keep at your proper distance,
Else we'll make you stare at our firm resistance,
Let alone the lads who are freedom tasting,
Recollect our dads gave you once a basting.

CHORUS
> Pickaxe, shovel, spade, crowbar, hoe and barrow,
> Better not invade, Yankees have the marrow!

To protect our rights against your flints and triggers,
See on yonder heights our patriotic diggers.
Men of every age, color, rank, profession,
Ardently engaged, labor in succession.

Grandeur leaves her towers, poverty her hovel,
Here to join their powers with the hoe and shovel,
Here the merchant toils with the patriotic sawyer,
There the laborer smiles, near him sweats the lawyer.

CHORUS

Scholars leave their schools, with their patriotic teachers,
Farmers seize their tools, headed by their preachers.
How they break the soil, brewers, butchers, bakers,
Here the doctors toil, there the undertakers.

Bright Apollo's sons leave their pipe and tabor,
Mid the roar of guns, join the martial labor,
Round the embattled plain in sweet concord rally,
And in freedom's strain sing the foe's finale.

CHORUS

Plumbers, founders, dyers, tinmen, turners, shavers,
Sweepers, clerks and criers, jewelers, engravers,
Clothiers, drapers, players, cartmen, hatters, tailors,
Gaugers, sealers, weighers, carpenters and sailors.

Better not invade, recollect the spirit
Which our dads displayed and their sons inherit,
If you still advance, friendly caution slighting,
You may get by chance a bellyful of fighting.

CHORUS

The Hunters of Kentucky

After Napoleon's defeat in 1814 the British sent 18,000 seasoned troops to Canada, ending American hopes of conquest there. On December 24, 1814, Britain and the United States signed a peace treaty in Ghent, Belgium. The greatest battle of the war took place at New Orleans, fifteen days after the peace treaty was signed. British General Packenham, invading New Orleans with an army of 8,000 men, encountered Andrew Jackson and his army of sharpshooters from Kentucky and Tennessee. The British suffered 2,000 casualties, Jackson lost 13 men. Samuel Woodworth ("Patriotic Diggers") wrote the words to "The Hunters of Kentucky," using the traditional folk melody "Miss Bailey's Ghost."

The Hunters of Kentucky

Words: Samuel Woodworth. Music: anonymous.

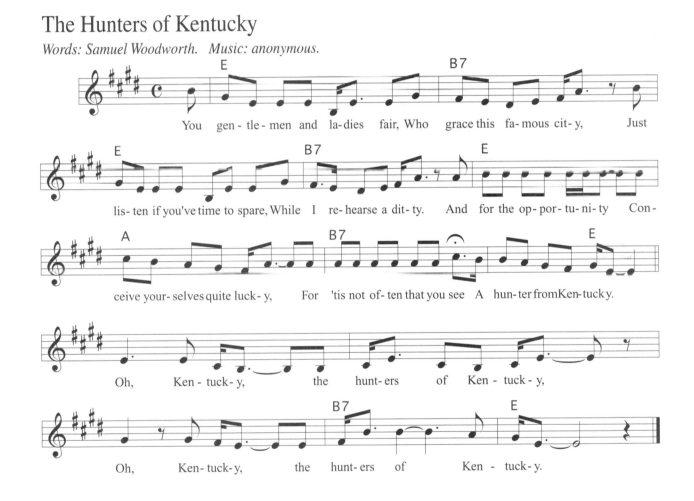

You gen-tle-men and la-dies fair, Who grace this fa-mous cit-y, Just lis-ten if you've time to spare, While I re-hearse a dit-ty. And for the op-por-tu-ni-ty Con-ceive your-selves quite luck-y, For 'tis not of-ten that you see A hun-ter from Ken-tuck-y. Oh, Ken-tuck-y, the hunt-ers of Ken-tuck-y, Oh, Ken-tuck-y, the hunt-ers of Ken-tuck-y.

You gentlemen and ladies fair,
Who grace this famous city,
Just listen if you've time to spare,
While I rehearse a ditty.
And for the opportunity
Conceive yourselves quite lucky,
For 'tis not often that you see
A hunter from Kentucky.

We are a hardy freeborn race,
Each man to fear a stranger,
Whate'er the game we join in chase,
Despising time and danger,
And if a daring foe annoys,
Whate'er his strength and forces,
We'll show him that Kentucky boys
Are alligator horses.

CHORUS
        Oh, Kentucky, the hunters of Kentucky,
        Oh, Kentucky, the hunters of Kentucky.

I suppose you've read it in the prints
How Packenham attempted,
To make Old Hickory Jackson wince,
But soon his scheme repented,
For we, with rifles ready cocked,
Thought such occasion lucky,
And soon around the general flocked
The hunters of Kentucky.

You've heard, I suppose, how New Orleans
Is famed for wealth and beauty,
There's girls of every hue it seems,
From snowy-white to sooty.
So Packenham he made his brags,
If he in fight was lucky,
He'd have their girls and cotton bags,
In spite of old Kentucky.

CHORUS

But Jackson he was wide awake,
And was not scared at trifles,
For well he knew what aim we take
With our Kentucky rifles.
So he led us down to Cypress swamp,
The ground was low and mucky,
There stood John Bull in martial pomp,
And here was old Kentucky.

A bank was raised to hide our breasts,
Not that we thought of dying,
But that we always like to rest,
Unless the game is flying.
Behind it stood our little force,
None wished it to be greater,
For every man was half a horse,
And half an alligator.

CHORUS

They did not let our patience tire,
Before they showed their faces,
We did not choose to waste our fire,
So snugly kept our places,
But when so near we saw them wink,
We thought it time to stop 'em,
And 'twould have done you good I think,
To see Kentuckians drop 'em.

They found, at last, 'twas vain to fight,
Where lead was all the booty,
And so they wisely took to flight,
And left us all our beauty.
And now, if danger e'er annoys,
Remember what our trade is,
Just send for us Kentucky boys,
And we'll protect you, ladies.

CHORUS

Andrew Jackson

The War of 1812 was a war filled with irony. One of the major causes of the war, interference with American shipping, was created by the British Orders in Council. These orders were repealed in England, two days before the United States declared war, but news did not reach America until after the war had begun. When the war ended, both sides claimed victory, and all land captured by either side was given up. The war did, however, stimulate a rapid increase in American manufacturing, and helped solidify a strong national feeling. In addition, two Americans who distinguished themselves in battle, Andrew Jackson and William Henry Harrison, later became presidents of the United States. With colonialism and two wars with Britain behind her, the new nation was ready to challenge the west.

The first Great Seal of the United States of America

Recommended sources for and about songs sung in Colonial America, The American Revolution and The War of 1812:

Ames, Russell. *The Story of American Folksong.* New York: Grosset and Dunlap, 1960.

Botkin, B. A. *A Treasury of New England Folklore.* New York: Crown Publishers, 1947.

Brand, Oscar. *Songs of '76, A Folksinger's History of the Revolution.* Philadelphia and New York: M. Evans and Company, Inc., 1972.

Bronson, Bertrand. *The Traditional Tunes of the Child Ballads* (four volumes). New Jersey: Princeton University Press, 1959-72.

Child, Francis James. *The English and Scottish Popular Ballads* (five volumes). New York: Dover, 1966.

Cole, William and Monath, Norman. *Folk Songs of England, Ireland, Scotland and Wales.* Garden City, New York: Doubleday & Company, 1961.

Dolph, Edward Arthur. *"Sound Off" Soldiers Songs.* New York: Cosmopolitan Book Corp., 1929.

Forcucci, Samuel L. *A Folk Song History of America.* Englewood Cliffs, New Jersey: Prentice- Hall, Inc., 1984.

Ives, Burl. *The Burl Ives Song Book.* New York: Ballantine Books, 1953.

Korson, George. *Pennsylvania Songs and Legends.* Philadelphia: University of Pennsylvania Press, 1949.

Krythe, Maymie R. *Sampler of American Songs.* New York, Evanston and London: Harper & Row, 1969.

Lochlainn, Colm O. *Irish Street Ballads.* New York: Corinth, 1960.

Lomax, Alan. *The Folk Songs of North America.* New York: Doubleday, 1960.

Raph, Theodore. *The Songs We Sang.* New York: A. S. Barnes and Co., 1964.

Scott, John Anthony. *The Ballad of America.* New York: Bantam, 1966.

Sharp, Cecil J. *English Folk Songs from the Southern Appalachians.* London: Oxford University Press, 1960.

Silber, Irwin. *Songs of Independence.* Stackpole Books, 1973.

Spaeth, Sigmund. *Read 'Em and Weep.* New York: Doubleday, Page & Company, 1926.

Vinson, Lee. *The Early American Songbook.* Englewood Cliffs, New Jersey: Prentice-Hall, 1974.

Warner, Anne. *Traditional American Folk Songs.* Syracuse University Press, 1984.

For Scots bagpipe music (marches, strathspeys, reels, retreats, slow marches and jigs): *Scots Guards Standard Settings of Pipe Music.* Paterson's Publications Ltd., 36 Wigmore Street, London, 1965.

For Irish fiddle tunes: (airs, jigs, reels, hornpipes, long dances and marches): *O'Neill's Music of Ireland, Eighteen Hundred and Fifty Melodies.* Bronx, New York: Daniel Michael Collins, 1903.

For psalms: a collection compiled by the Church of Scotland, the United Free Church of Scotland and the Presbyterian churches of Australia, New Zealand and South Africa entitled: *The Psalter in Metre and Church Hymnary With Music.* London, Edinburgh, Glasgow, Copenhagen, New York, Toronto, Melbourne, Cape Town, Bombay, Calcutta, Madras, Shanghai: Oxford University Press, 1924.

For recordings: *Colonial & Revolution Songs with historical narration.* WEM Records, 16230 Van Buren Blvd., Riverside, California, 92504, 1989.

Picture Credits

Index of Song Titles